What Can We Do About ENDANGERED ANIMALS?

Suzanne Slade

PowerKiDS press.

New York

To the awesome Wagner family—Tim, Kathryn, Forrest, Jeffrey, and Matt

Published in 2010 by The Rosen Publishing Group, Inc.
29 East 21st Street, New York, NY 10010

First Edition

Editor: Amelie von Zumbusch
Book Design: Kate Laczynski
Photo Researcher: Jessica Gerweck

Photo Credits: Back cover graphic © www.istockphoto.com/Jan Rysavy; cover, pp. 1, 4, 12 Shutterstock.com; back cover earth graphic © www.istockphoto.com/Jan Rysavy; p. 6 © Joseph Van Os/Getty Images; p. 8 © Jeff Foott/Getty Images; p. 10 © Frans Lanting/Corbis; p. 14 © Norbert Wu/Getty Images; p. 16 © Keren Su/Corbis; p. 18 © Daniel J. Cox/Getty Images; p. 20 © Reuters/Corbis.

Library of Congress Cataloging-in-Publication Data

Slade, Suzanne.
  What can we do about endangered animals? / Suzanne Slade.
     p. cm. — (Protecting our planet)
  Includes index.
  ISBN 978-1-4042-8080-9 (library binding) — ISBN 978-1-4358-2477-5 (pbk.) — ISBN 978-1-4358-2478-2 (6-pack)
  1. Endangered species—Juvenile literature. 2. Wildlife conservation—Juvenile literature. I. Title.
  QL83.S58 2010
  333.95'42—dc22
                                        2008048151

Manufactured in the United States of America

CPSIA Compliance Information: Batch #WRW909101PK: For Further Information contact Rosen Publishing, New York, New York at 1-800-237-9932

CONTENTS

Orangutans are endangered both because the forests where they live are being cut down and because people hunt them.

Wonderful Animals

We share our world with **millions** of wonderful animals. Some kinds of animals, such as red wolves, Cuban crocodiles, sea otters, and blue whales, are endangered. This means that they are in danger of becoming **extinct**, or disappearing forever. Sadly, several kinds of animals become extinct every day!

The main reason animals are disappearing is people. For hundreds of years, people have hunted animals for sport and food. We have also destroyed animal homes and **polluted** the land, air, and water where animals live. Luckily, many people are now working to help endangered animals. Together we can save Earth's beautiful animals.

Some conservation groups list animals that need protection as critically endangered, endangered, or vulnerable. Clouded leopards are vulnerable.

Conservationists keep a close watch on animals in danger. They carefully consider which ones should be placed on lists so governments can help **protect** them. In the United States, animals that are very close to becoming extinct are put on the endangered **species** list. Endangered animals, such as gray bats and sea turtles, need new laws to protect them and the places where they live.

Some animals are close to becoming endangered but are still greater in number than endangered animals are. The U.S. government lists these animals as threatened. Threatened animals also receive special care and protection.

DID YOU KNOW?

Animals that are listed as extinct in the wild no longer live in the wild but are still found in places such as zoos and wildlife centers. Totally extinct animals are gone forever.

Whooping cranes move with the seasons. People can help these endangered birds by protecting land along their paths.

Habitats Are Homes

Animals live in different **habitats** all over the world. Animals find food, places to hide from enemies, and protection from bad weather in their habitats. Through the years, though, people have destroyed many habitats. Green, leafy forests were chopped down for wood. **Wetlands** were filled in with dirt to make new farmland. Quiet deserts became busy cities with new houses and roads.

An animal is put in danger when its habitat disappears. For example, when some Florida wetlands were turned into farms, hundreds of whooping cranes lost their habitats. Some cranes found new homes, but those who could not died.

People hunt black rhinoceroses mostly for their horns. Only a few thousand of these endangered animals are left.

The Hunted

Other animals become endangered due to hunting. Long ago, people hunted animals mainly for food. People also made clothing from animal skins. Today, many hunters kill animals for sport, or fun. Hunters enjoy being out in nature as they search for animals. However, sometimes hunters kill too many animals.

Red wolves, black-footed ferrets, and black rhinoceroses are a few of the animals that are endangered due to overhunting. Luckily, special laws now protect all three animals. As a result, these mighty animals are becoming more plentiful every year.

DID YOU KNOW?

At one time, more than one-fourth of all birds in the United States were passenger pigeons. In the 1800s, hunters killed huge numbers of pigeons. In 1914, the last passenger pigeon died.

12

Scientists think that seabirds, such as this albatross, are
among the animals most in danger from global warming.

Our Changing Climate

Different parts of the world have different climates. A place's climate is the **temperature** and amount of rainfall that place has most of the time. The climate in a certain place greatly affects the plants and animals that can live there.

Lately, people and the pollution they make have caused Earth's overall climate to become warmer. This rise in temperature is called **global warming**. Global warming has made ice sheets at the North Pole and South Pole melt, which has caused seawater to rise. Conservationists fear that the warming climate is endangering elephants, great apes, polar bears, birds, and many other animals.

Scientists think sea turtles may swallow plastic bags because
they look like the jellyfish that many sea turtles eat.

The Dangers of Pollution

Even without global warming, pollution would still be a danger to many animals. Littering alone kills thousands of animals every year. Sea animals choke on bags people throw in the ocean. Birds die from eating trash on the beach.

Chemicals hurt animals, too. Years ago, farmers used a chemical called DDT to kill bugs that ate their crops. Peregrine falcons dined on animals that ate bugs covered with DDT. Bald eagles ate fish from rivers polluted with DDT. The DDT then caused many falcon and eagle eggs to break before they could **hatch**. As a result, both of these birds became endangered.

Like several of the remaining wild giant pandas, this animal lives in China's Wolong National Nature Reserve.

Protecting Pandas

One of the world's most popular animals is the giant panda. This peaceful bear lives in the mountains of southwest China. Sadly, many giant pandas disappeared when their forest habitats were cut down. Hunters also illegally killed these bears for fur.

Conservationists are working to save the 1,600 remaining pandas in the wild. There are now 6,000 square miles (15,540 sq km) of forests protected from saws and hunters. The pandas and cubs living in these protected forests can now climb, play, and grow up safely.

DID YOU KNOW?

The giant panda's main food is a tall, woody grass, called bamboo. One giant panda can munch 26 to 83 pounds (12–38 kg) of bamboo a day. Conservationists are also working to protect bamboo forests.

Florida panthers, such as this powerful animal, are
the biggest wild cats in the eastern United States.

Saving Panthers

Not long ago, hundreds of panthers lived in Texas, Alabama, Mississippi, Arkansas, Louisiana, Georgia, and Tennessee. However, new houses destroyed much of their habitat and many of these big cats died. Hunters killed panthers, too. By the 1970s, there were only about 20 panthers, all of which lived in Florida.

People have taken action to help Florida panthers. Some panthers were moved into **captivity**, where they could stay safe. People began protecting the panther's forest and wetland habitats. By working together, people have helped the number of Florida panthers grow. Today, there are more than 100 panthers in the wild!

Many groups help animals. These International Fund for Animal Welfare members are cleaning oil off a pelican.

Working Together

When people work together with others, they can make a big difference in saving Earth's endangered animals. Many people join nature **organizations** to help animals in danger.

The world's largest nature organization is the World Wildlife Fund, or WWF. WWF works in 100 countries and has about five million members. The National Wildlife Federation protects and rebuilds American habitats and cares for the animals that live in them. The U.S. Fish and Wildlife Service is a government group that keeps a list of endangered and threatened animals. This group also works to save animals and their habitats.

You Can Help Animals

Caring people have helped many endangered animals. When the bald eagle was named America's national bird in 1782, thousands of these proud birds filled the skies. By the 1960s, fewer than 1,000 birds remained, due to habitat loss and hunting. The government quickly passed laws to protect these birds. Today, there are more than 20,000 bald eagles!

You can help animals, too. Joining a nature organization is a great way to make new friends and help wildlife. You can also help animals by keeping their habitats clean. Pick up trash in your neighborhood. Help cut pollution by walking instead of riding in a car. It feels good to help our animals!

GLOSSARY

captivity (kap-TIH-vih-tee) A place where animals live, such as in a home, a zoo, or an aquarium, instead of living in the wild.

chemicals (KEH-mih-kulz) Matter that can be mixed with other matter to cause changes.

conservationists (kon-ser-VAY-shun-ists) People who want to keep nature safe.

extinct (ek-STINKT) No longer existing.

global warming (GLOH-bul WARM-ing) A raising of Earth's temperature. It is caused by gases that are let out when people burn fuels, such as gasoline.

habitats (HA-beh-tats) The kinds of land where certain animals or plants naturally live.

hatch (HACH) To come out of an egg.

millions (MIL-yunz) Thousands of thousands.

organizations (or-guh-nuh-ZAY-shunz) Groups.

polluted (puh-LOOT-ed) Poisoned with harmful matter.

protect (pruh-TEKT) To keep safe.

species (SPEE-sheez) One kind of living thing. All people are one species.

temperature (TEM-pur-chur) How hot or cold something is.

wetlands (WET-landz) Land with a lot of wetness in the soil.

INDEX

WEB SITES

Due to the changing nature of Internet links, PowerKids Press has developed an online list of Web sites related to the subject of this book. This site is updated regularly. Please use this link to access the list:

www.powerkidslinks.com/ourpl/dangeran/